HAL•LEONARD

PIANO VOCAL GUITAR

ESSENTIAL SONGS

The 1920s

ISBN 0-634-09290-1

HAL•LEONARD®
CORPORATION
7777 W. BLUEMOUND RD. P.O. BOX 13819 MILWAUKEE, WI 53213

Visit Hal Leonard Online at
www.halleonard.com

CONTENTS

AIN'T MISBEHAVIN'

from AIN'T MISBEHAVIN'

Words by ANDY RAZAF
Music by THOMAS "FATS" WALLER
and HARRY BROOKS

ALABAMY BOUND
from THE GREAT AMERICAN BROADCAST

Words by B.G. DeSYLVA and BUD GREEN
Music by RAY HENDERSON

Moderately fast

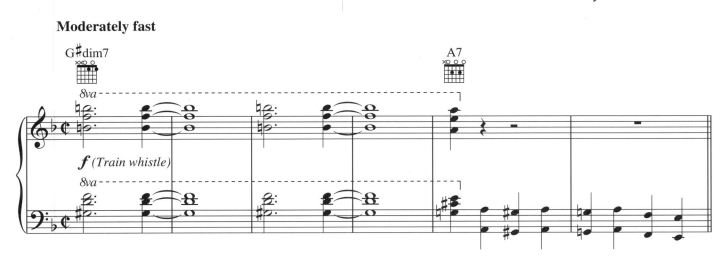

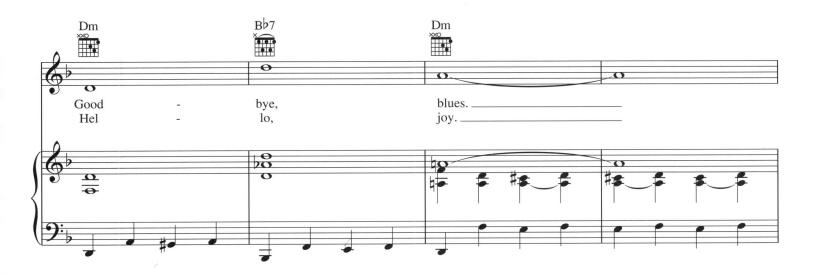

Good - bye,   blues. _____
Hel - lo,   joy. _____

Bird - ies are sing - in' ev - 'ry old thing in   tune. _____
Nev - er knew I would, nev - er knew I could   smile. _____

AIN'T SHE SWEET

Words by JACK YELLEN
Music by MILTON AGER

AIN'T WE GOT FUN?

from BY THE LIGHT OF THE SILVERY MOON

Words by GUS KAHN and RAYMOND B. EGAN
Music by RICHARD A. WHITING

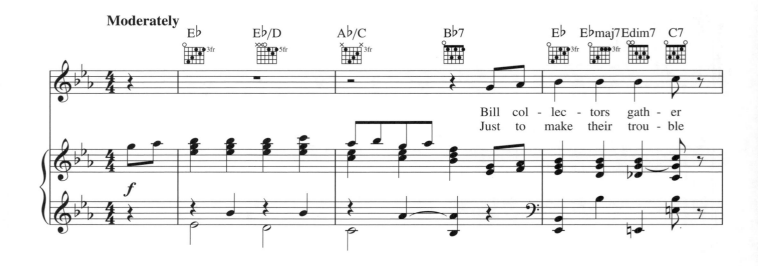

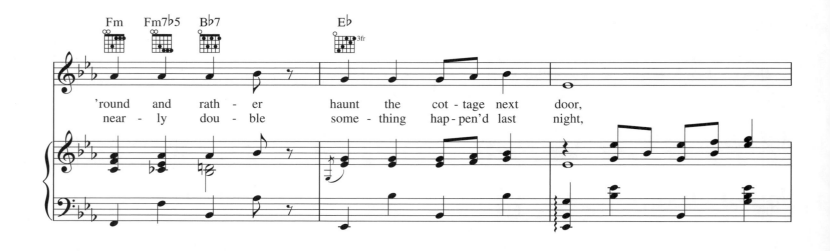

ALL ALONE

Words and Music by IRVING BERLIN

Just like a mel-o-dy that lin - gers on,
Just for a mo-ment you were mine, and then

ALL BY MYSELF

Words and Music by
IRVING BERLIN

ALWAYS

Words and Music by
IRVING BERLIN

Ev-'ry - thing went wrong, and the whole day
Dreams will all come true, grow - ing old with

long _____ I'd feel so
you, _____ and time will

AMONG MY SOUVENIRS

Words by EDGAR LESLIE
Music by HORATIO NICHOLLS

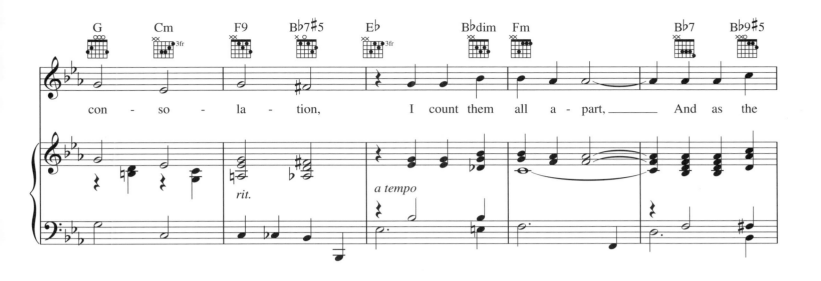

con - so - la - tion, I count them all a - part, _____ And as the

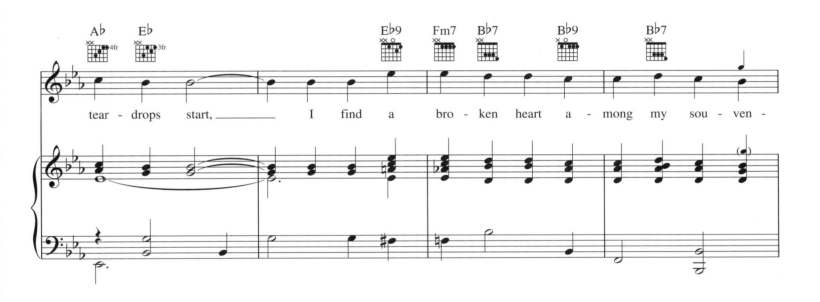

tear - drops start, _____ I find a bro - ken heart a - mong my sou - ven -

irs. _____   irs. _____

ANGRY

Words by DUDLEY MECUM
Music by JULES CASSARD, HENRY BRUNIES and MERRITT BRUNIES

APRIL SHOWERS

from BOMBO

Words by B.G. DeSYLVA
Music by LOUIS SILVERS

With an easy flow

AVALON

Words by AL JOLSON and B.G. DeSYLVA
Music by VINCENT ROSE

Moderately

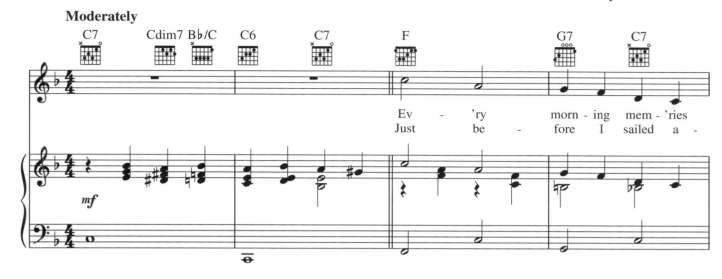

Ev - 'ry morn - ing mem - 'ries
Just be - fore I sailed a -

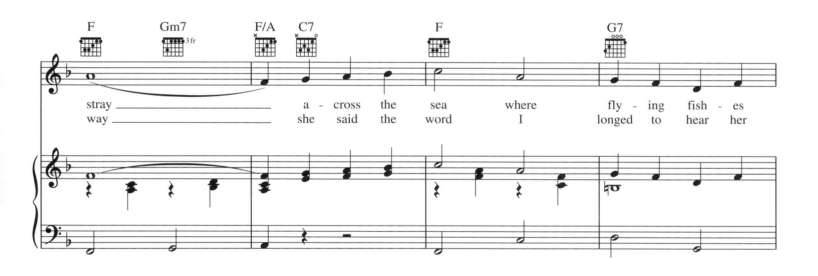

stray ___ a - cross the sea where fly - ing fish - es
way ___ she said the word I longed to hear her

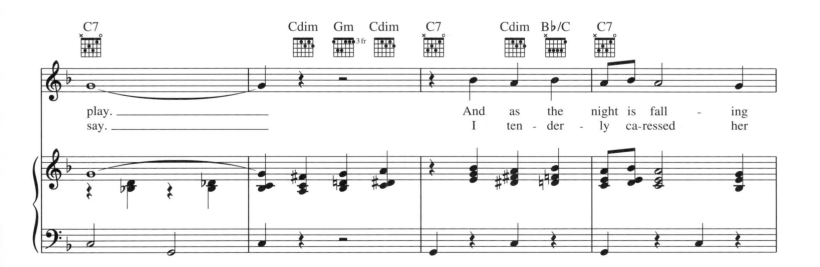

play. ___ And as the night is fall - ing
say. ___ I ten - der - ly ca-ressed her

AT SUNDOWN

Words and Music by
WALTER DONALDSON

46

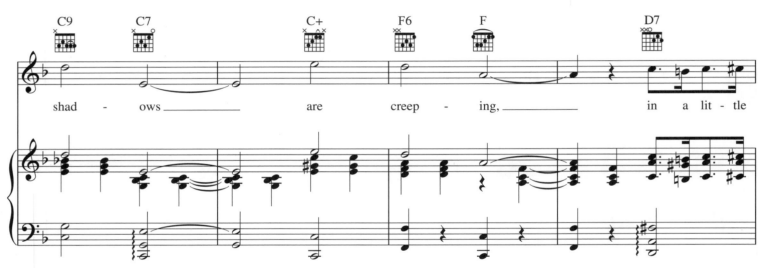

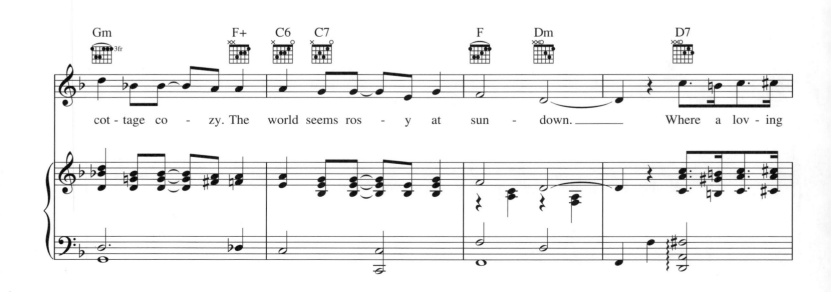

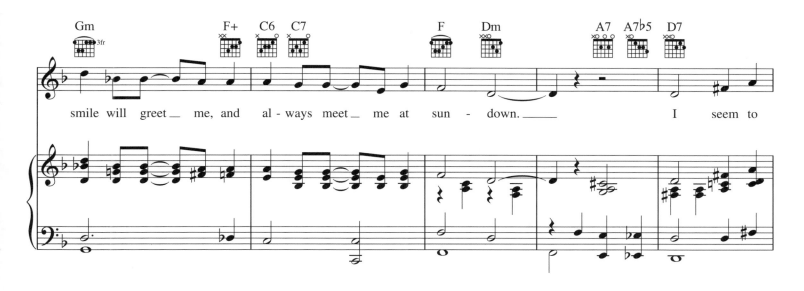

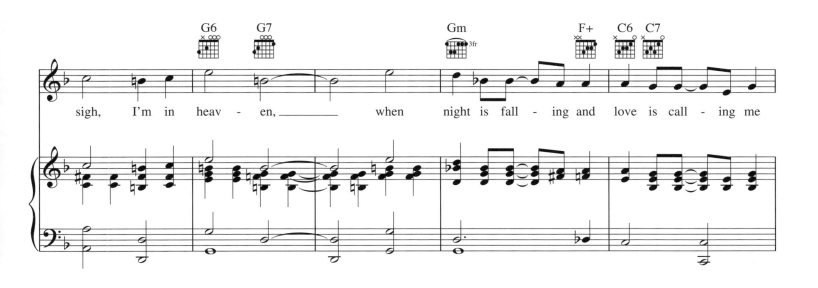

BASIN STREET BLUES

Words and Music by
SPENCER WILLIAMS

Moderately

THE BEST THINGS IN LIFE ARE FREE

from GOOD NEWS!

Music and Lyrics by B.G. DeSYLVA,
LEW BROWN and RAY HENDERSON

BILL

from SHOW BOAT

Music by JEROME KERN
Words by P.G. WODEHOUSE
and OSCAR HAMMERSTEIN II

54

THE BIRTH OF THE BLUES
from GEORGE WHITE'S SCANDALS OF 1926

Words by B.G. DeSYLVA and LEW BROWN
Music by RAY HENDERSON

THE BLUE ROOM
from THE GIRL FRIEND

Words by LORENZ HART
Music by RICHARD RODGERS

BLUE SKIES
from BETSY

Words and Music by
IRVING BERLIN

BUTTON UP YOUR OVERCOAT

from FOLLOW THRU

Words and Music by B.G. DeSYLVA,
LEW BROWN and RAY HENDERSON

BYE BYE BLACKBIRD

from PETE KELLY'S BLUES

Lyric by MORT DIXON
Music by RAY HENDERSON

73

CALIFORNIA, HERE I COME

Words and Music by AL JOLSON,
B.G. DeSYLVA and JOSEPH MEYER

76

CAN'T HELP LOVIN' DAT MAN

from SHOW BOAT

Lyrics by OSCAR HAMMERSTEIN II
Music by JEROME KERN

Slowly

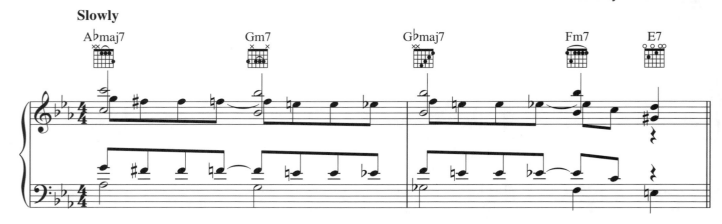

Fish got to swim ___ and birds got to fly, ___ I got to love ___ one
Tell me he's la - zy, tell me he's slow, ___ tell me I'm cra - zy,

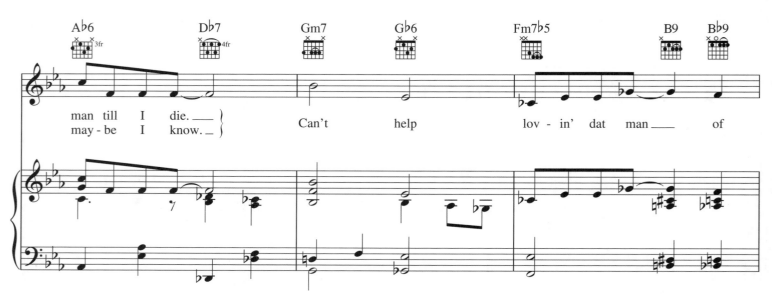

man till I die. ___ }
may - be I know. ___ }
Can't help lov - in' dat man ___ of

CAROLINA IN THE MORNING

Lyrics by GUS KAHN
Music by WALTER DONALDSON

CAROLINA MOON

Lyric by BENNY DAVIS
Music by JOE BURKE

CHARMAINE

Words and Music by
LEW POLLACK and ERNO RAPEE

CHICAGO
(That Toddlin' Town)

Words and Music by
FRED FISHER

DOWN YONDER

Words and Music by
L. WOLFE GILBERT

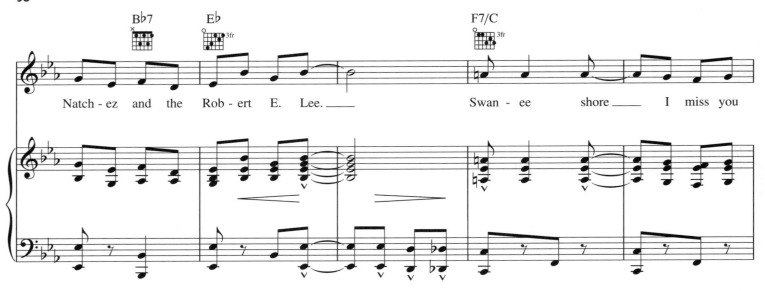

Natch - ez and the Rob - ert E. Lee. _____ Swan - ee shore _____ I miss you

more and more, _____ ev - 'ry day, my mam - my land, you're sim -

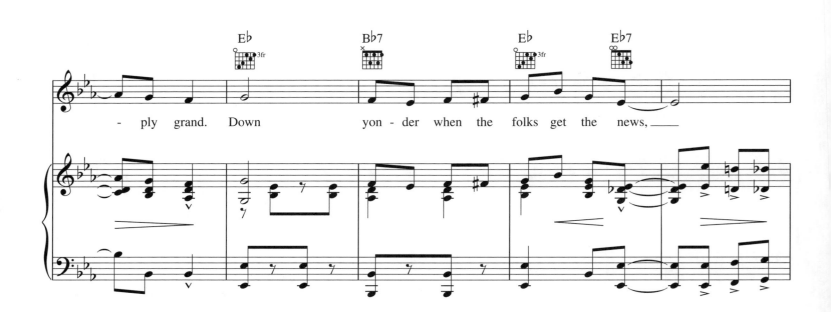

- ply grand. Down yon - der when the folks get the news, _____

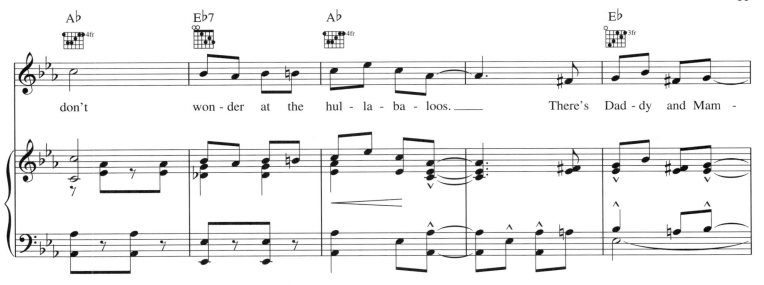

don't won-der at the hul-la-ba-loos.____ There's Dad-dy and Mam -

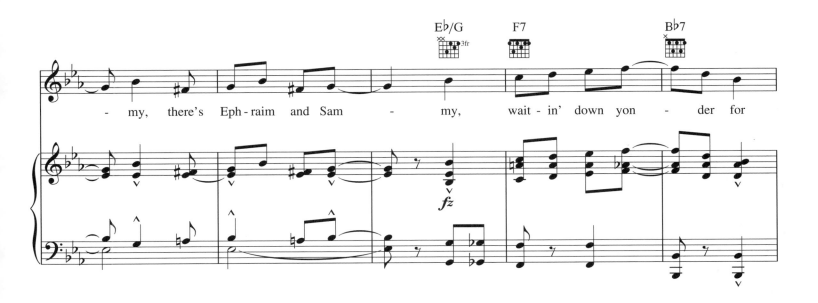

- my, there's Eph-raim and Sam - my, wait-in' down yon - der for

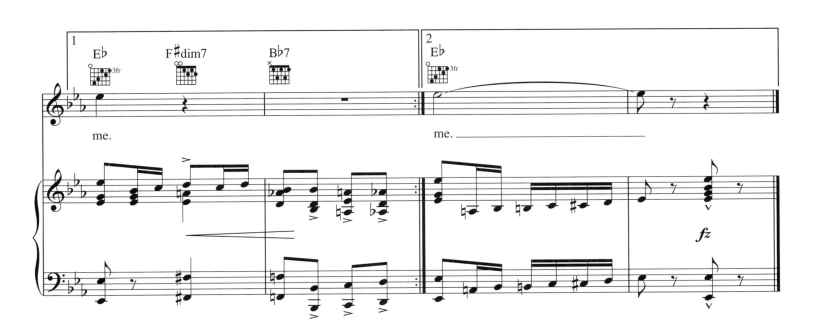

me.

me.____

'DEED I DO

Words and Music by WALTER HIRSCH
and FRED ROSE

EVERYBODY LOVES MY BABY
(But My Baby Don't Love Nobody But Me)

Words and Music by
JACK PALMER and SPENCER WILLIAMS

With a beat

VERSE

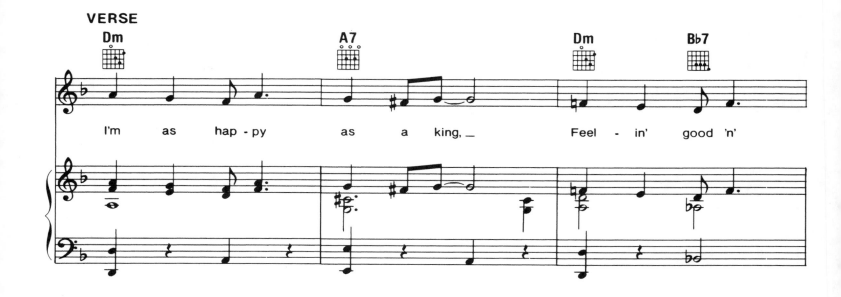

I'm as hap-py as a king, __ Feel - in' good 'n'

ev - 'ry-thing. __ I'm just like a bird in Spring, __

107

FAR ABOVE CAYUGA'S WATERS

Words and Music by
C. URGUHART

FIVE FOOT TWO, EYES OF BLUE
(Has Anybody Seen My Girl?)

Words by JOE YOUNG and SAM LEWIS
Music by RAY HENDERSON

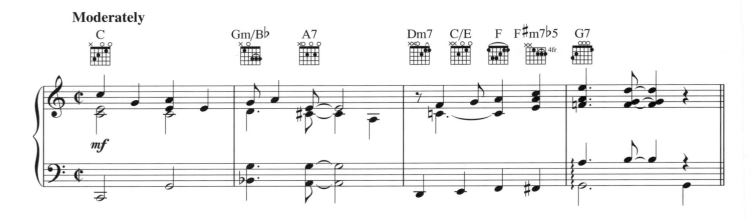

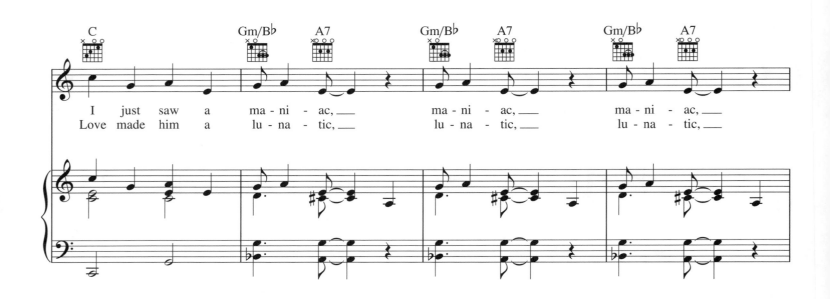

I just saw a ma-ni-ac, ___ ma-ni-ac, ___ ma-ni-ac, ___
Love made him a lu-na-tic, ___ lu-na-tic, ___ lu-na-tic, ___

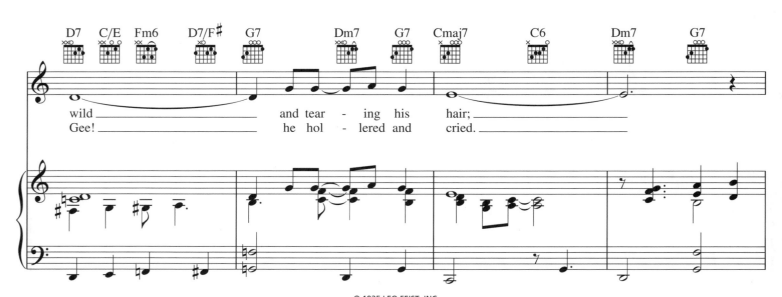

wild ___ and tear-ing his hair; ___
Gee! ___ he hol-lered and cried. ___

GEE BABY, AIN'T I GOOD TO YOU

Words by DON REDMAN and ANDY RAZAF
Music by DON REDMAN

To Coda ⊕

way _____ that I do. Gee ba-by, ain't I good _____ to

you!

you!

Lis - ten, ___ lis -ten to what I have to say, ___ what I want to tell

you, lis - ten, ___ lis -ten to why I feel this way, ___

HERE COMES THE SHOW BOAT

Words by BILLY ROSE
Music by MACEO PINKARD

Medium Fox tempo

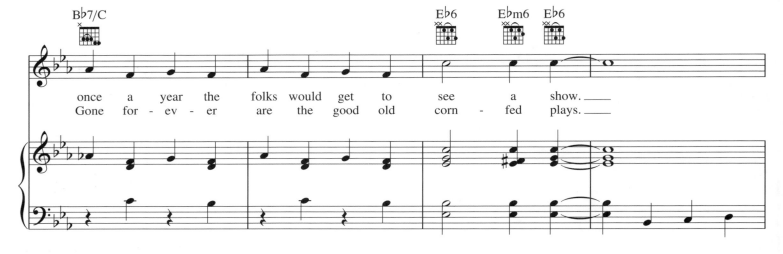

On the Mis-sis-sip-pi fif-ty years a-go, ___
Gone for-ev-er are the cot-ton blos-som days. ___

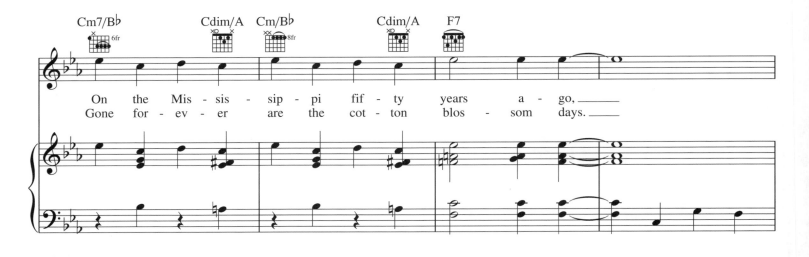

once a year the folks would get to see a show. ___
Gone for-ev-er are the good old corn - fed plays. ___

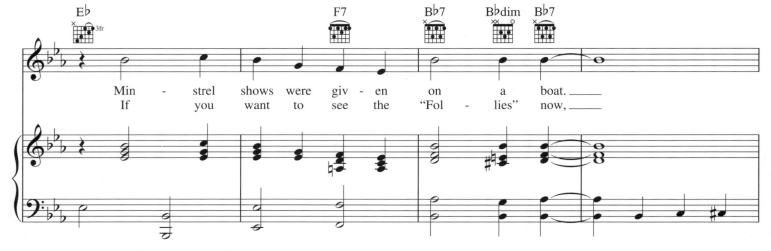

Min - strel shows were giv-en on a boat. ___
If you want to see the "Fol - lies" now, ___

HONEY

Words and Music by RICHARD WHITING,
SEYMOUR SIMONS and HAVEN GILLESPIE

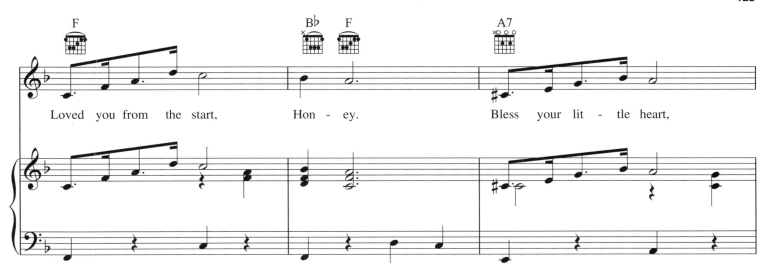

Loved you from the start, Hon - ey. Bless your lit - tle heart,

Hon - ey. Ev - 'ry day would be so sun - ny,

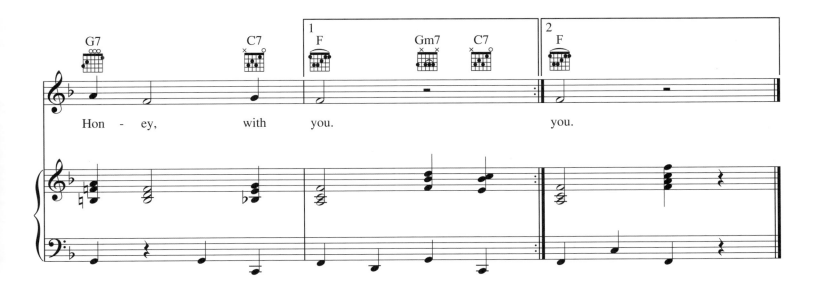

Hon - ey, with you. you.

I CAN'T BELIEVE THAT YOU'RE IN LOVE WITH ME

Words and Music by JIMMY McHUGH
and CLARENCE GASKILL

Yes - ter - day you came my way. And when you smiled at
Skies are gray, I'm blue each day. When you are not a -

me, in my heart I felt a thrill. _____ You
round, ev - 'ry - thing goes wrong, my dear, _____ I've

I CAN'T GIVE YOU ANYTHING BUT LOVE

from BLACKBIRDS OF 1928

By JIMMY McHUGH
and DOROTHY FIELDS

Gee, but it's tough to be broke, kid. _____ It's not a joke, kid, it's a

Rome was-n't built in a day, kid. _____ You have to pay, kid, for what you

curse.

get.

My luck is chang - ing, it's got - ten _____ from sim - ply

But I am will - ing to wait, dear, _____ your lit - tle

I CRIED FOR YOU

Words and Music by ARTHUR FREED,
GUS ARNHEIM and ABE LYMAN

I LOVE MY BABY
(My Baby Loves Me)

Words by BUD GREEN
Music by HARRY WARREN

I WANNA BE LOVED BY YOU

from GOOD BOY

Lyric by BERT KALMAR
Music by HERBERT STOTHART and HARRY RUBY

140

141

I'LL GET BY
(As Long as I Have You)

Lyric by ROY TURK
Music by FRED E. AHLERT

This old world was just as sad a place for me ___ as could be, ___
Since we met my life is full of hap-pi - ness, ___ and I guess, ___

Dm
D7
G7
there be rain and dark - ness too,
G7#5
I'll not com - plain, I'll
C
C#dim7
Dm7
G7
C
laugh it through. Pov - er - ty
G7
C
E7
E7#5
may come to me that's

146

IF YOU KNEW SUSIE
(Like I Know Susie)

Words and Music by B.G. DeSYLVA
and JOSEPH MEYER

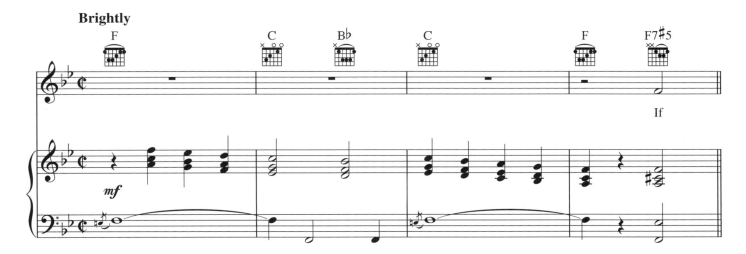

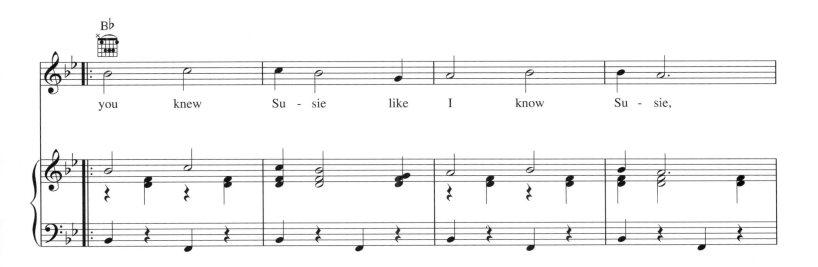

you knew Su - sie like I know Su - sie,

oh,   oh,   oh, what a girl! _____   There's / She

148

I'M LOOKING OVER
A FOUR LEAF CLOVER

Lyric by MORT DIXON
Music by HARRY WOODS

I'M SITTING ON TOP OF THE WORLD
from THE JOLSON STORY

Words by SAM M. LEWIS and JOE YOUNG
Music by RAY HENDERSON

I'VE FOUND A NEW BABY
(I Found a New Baby)

Words and Music by
JACK PALMER and SPENCER WILLIAMS

159

IN A LITTLE SPANISH TOWN

('Twas on a Night Like This)

Words by SAM M. LEWIS and JOE YOUNG
Music by MABEL WAYNE

Chorus, Slowly with much expression

In A Lit - tle Span - ish Town, 'Twas on a night like this, _____

Stars were peek - a - boo - ing down, 'Twas on a night like this, _____

I whis - pered "Be true to me," _____ And she

sighed: "Si, Si." _____

INDIAN LOVE CALL
from ROSE-MARIE

Lyrics by OTTO HARBACH and OSCAR HAMMERSTEIN II
Music by RUDOLF FRIML

166

IT ALL DEPENDS ON YOU
from THE SINGING FOOL

Words and Music by B.G. DeSYLVA,
LEW BROWN and RAY HENDERSON

LAST NIGHT ON THE BACK PORCH
(I Loved Her Best of All)

Words and Music by LEW BROWN
and CARL SCHRAUBSTADER

Brightly, but not too fast

There's a girl I'm wild a-bout. ___
time that she's a-lone ___

___ Ev-'ry time I take her out ___
___ when I call her on the phone, ___

LET A SMILE BE YOUR UMBRELLA

Words by IRVING KAHAL and FRANCIS WHEELER
Music by SAMMY FAIN

LIMEHOUSE BLUES
from ZIEGFELD FOLLIES

Words by DOUGLAS FURBER
Music by PHILIP BRAHAM

LINGER AWHILE

Lyric by LARRY OWENS
Music by VINCENT ROSE

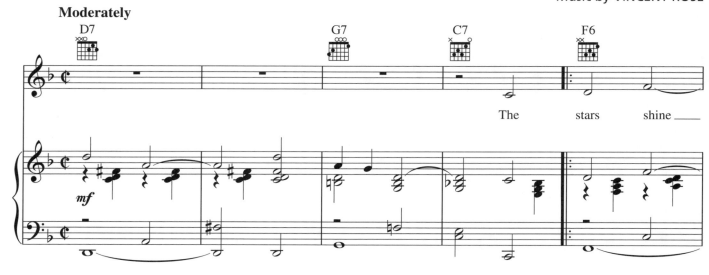

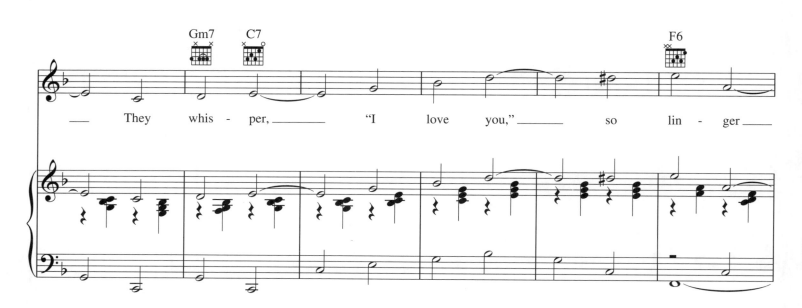

LOOK FOR THE SILVER LINING

from SALLY

Words by BUDDY DeSYLVA
Music by JEROME KERN

Refrain *(slowly, with warm expression)*

THE LOVE NEST

Words by OTTO HARBACH
Music by LOUIS A. HIRSCH

LOUISE

from the Paramount Picture INNOCENTS OF PARIS

Words by LEO ROBIN
Music by RICHARD A. WHITING

LOVE ME OR LEAVE ME

from LOVE ME OR LEAVE ME

Lyrics by GUS KAHN
Music by WALTER DONALDSON

LOVER, COME BACK TO ME

from THE NEW MOON

Lyrics by OSCAR HAMMERSTEIN II
Music by SIGMUND ROMBERG

Moderately fast Swing

The sky was blue, and high a-bove, Love had its day.
You came at last.

* *Recorded a half step higher.*
** *Play chord 1st time only.*

200

202

MAKE BELIEVE

from SHOW BOAT

Lyrics by OSCAR HAMMERSTEIN II
Music by JEROME KERN

MAKIN' WHOOPEE!
from WHOOPEE!

Lyrics by GUS KAHN
Music by WALTER DONALDSON

213

MANHATTAN

from the Broadway Musical THE GARRICK GAIETIES

Words by LORENZ HART
Music by RICHARD RODGERS

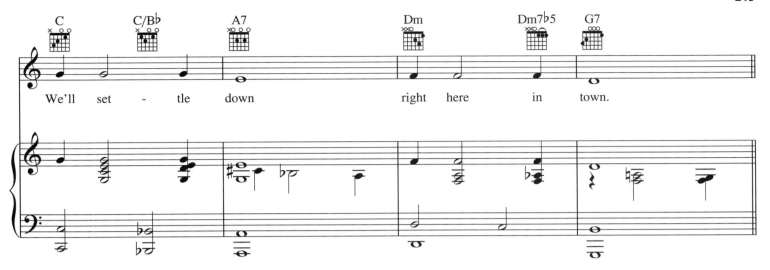

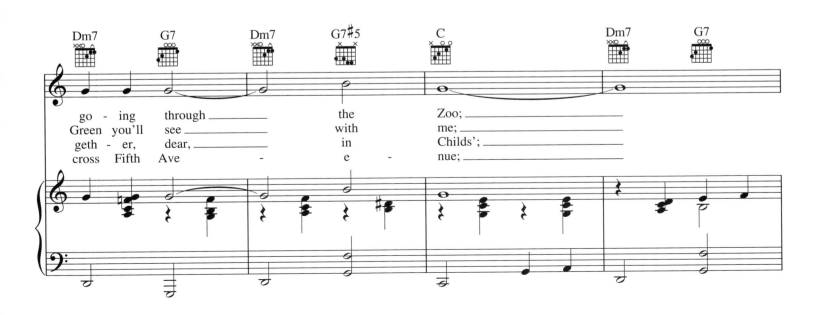

It's ver-y fan-cy on old De-lan-cey Street, you know;_____ The sub-way
We'll bathe at Brigh-ton the fist you'll fright-en when you're in;_____ Your bath-ing
We'll go to Co-ney and eat bo-lo-gna on a roll;_____ In Cen-tral
As black as on-yx we'll find the Bron-nix Park Ex-press;_____ Our Flat-bush

charms us so,_____ when balm-y breez-es blow to and fro; And tell me what street
suit so thin_____ will make the shell-fish grin fin to fin; I'd like to take a
Park, we'll stroll_____ where our first kiss we stole, soul to soul; And for some high fare
flat, I guess_____ will be a great suc-cess. More or less; A short va-ca-tion

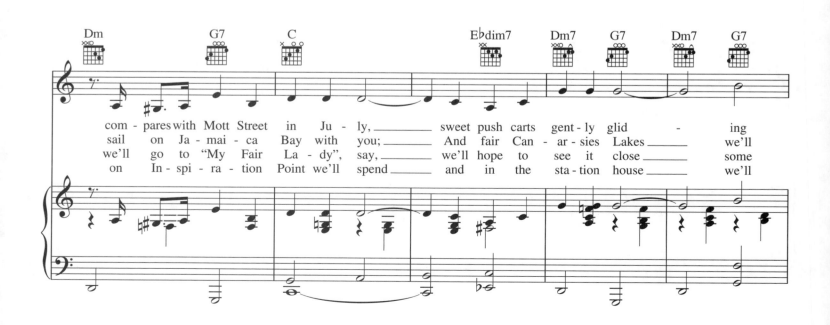

com - pares with Mott Street in Ju - ly,_____ sweet push carts gent-ly glid - ing
sail on Ja-mai-ca Bay with you;_____ And fair Can - ar-sies Lakes_____ we'll
we'll go to "My Fair La-dy", say,_____ we'll hope to see it close_____ some
on In-spi-ra-tion Point we'll spend_____ and in the sta-tion house_____ we'll

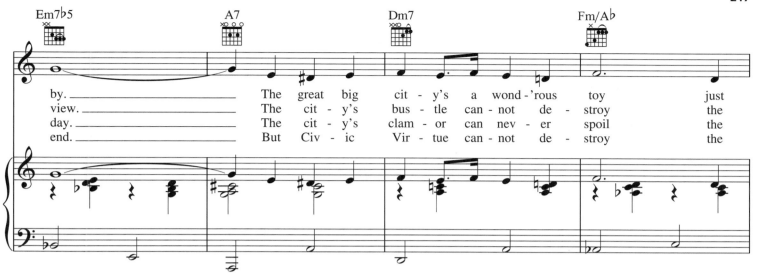

The great big cit-y's a wond-'rous toy just
The cit-y's bus-tle can-not de-stroy the
The cit-y's clam-or can nev-er spoil the
But Civ-ic Vir-tue can-not de-stroy the

made for a girl and boy.
dreams of a girl and boy.
dreams of a boy and goil.
dreams of a girl and boy.

We'll turn Man-hat-tan in-to an isle of

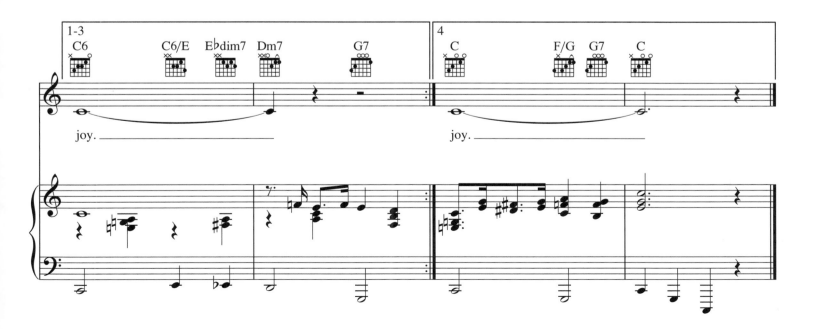

joy.

joy.

MARIE
from the Motion Picture THE AWAKENING

Words and Music by
IRVING BERLIN

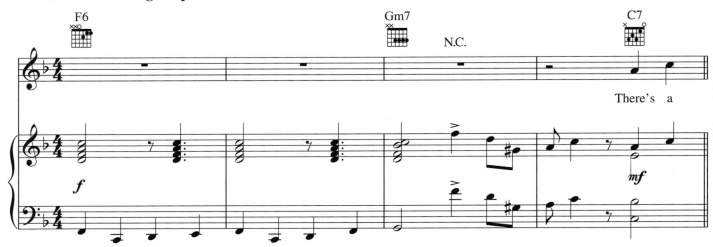

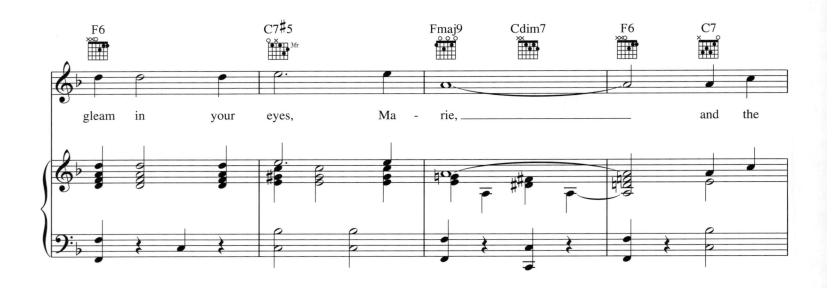

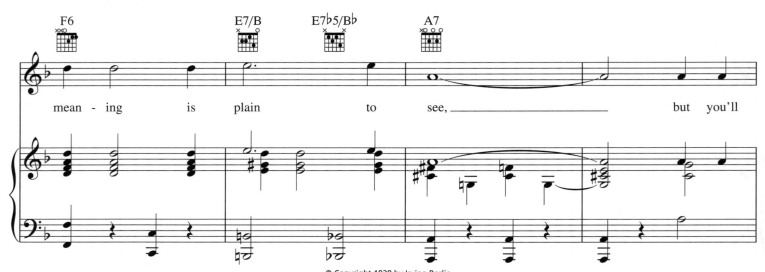

MEXICALI ROSE

from MEXICALI ROSE

Words by HELEN STONE
Music by JACK B. TENNEY

Mex - i - cal - i Rose, stop cry - ing;

I'll come back to you some sun - ny day. _____

Ev - 'ry night you'll know that I'll be pin - ing,

MISSISSIPPI MUD

Words and Music by JAMES CAVANAUGH
and HARRY BARRIS

225

MOONLIGHT AND ROSES
(Bring Mem'ries of You)

Words and Music by BEN BLACK,
EDWIN H. LEMARE and NEIL MORET

MOUNTAIN GREENERY

from the Broadway Musical THE GARRICK GAIETIES

Words by LORENZ HART
Music by RICHARD RODGERS

MY BLUE HEAVEN

Lyric by GEORGE WHITING
Music by WALTER DONALDSON

Day is end - ing, birds are wend - ing back to the shel - ter
Moon - beams creep - ing, flow'rs are sleep - ing un - der a star - lit

of each lit - tle nest they love. Night shades fall - ing,
way, wait - ing an - oth - er day. Time for rest - ing,

MY BUDDY

Lyrics by GUS KAHN
Music by WALTER DONALDSON

Life is a book that we stud-y _____ some of its leaves bring a
Bud-dies thru all of the gay days _____ bud-dies when some-thing went

sigh. _____ There it was writ-ten my Bud-dy _____
wrong, _____ I wait a - lone thru the gray days _____

MY MAN

Words and Music by JAMES HANLEY
and GENE BUCK

MY HEART STOOD STILL
from A CONNECTICUT YANKEE

Words by LORENZ HART
Music by RICHARD RODGERS

MY LUCKY STAR

Words and Music by B.G. DeSYLVA,
LEW BROWN and RAY HENDERSON

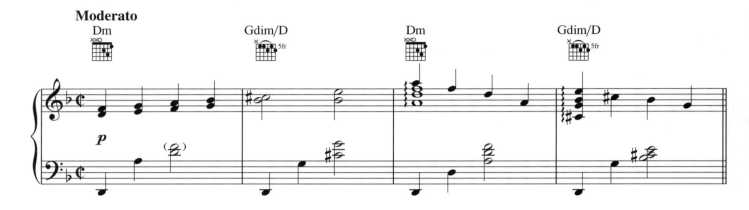

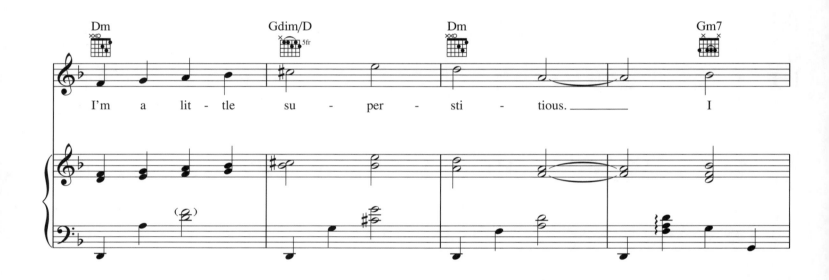

I'm a lit-tle su-per-sti-tious. _____ I

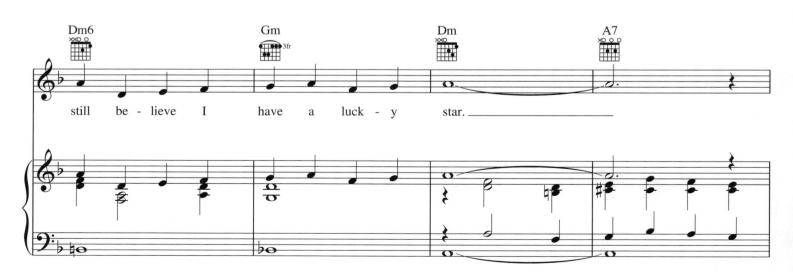

still be-lieve I have a luck-y star. _____

255

OL' MAN RIVER

from SHOW BOAT

Lyrics by OSCAR HAMMERSTEIN II
Music by JEROME KERN

ROCKIN' CHAIR

Words and Music by
HOAGY CARMICHAEL

PADDLIN' MADELIN' HOME

Words and Music by
HARRY WOODS

midnight on the riv - er, I heard her fa - ther call. But

pet - ted in the par - lor, and hugged her in the hall. But

she don't care, and I don't care, if we get back at all: } 'Cause when I'm

when she's out in my ca - noe I love her best of all: } 'Cause when I'm

pad - dl - in' Ma - de - lin' home, _____ Gee! when I'm

pad - dl - in' Ma - de - lin' home, _____ { first I
{ first I

PUTTIN' ON THE RITZ
from the Motion Picture PUTTIN' ON THE RITZ

Words and Music by
IRVING BERLIN

ST. LOUIS BLUES

from BIRTH OF THE BLUES

Words and Music by
W.C. HANDY

276

Extra Choruses (optional)

Lawd, a blonde-headed woman makes a good man leave the town,
I said a blonde-headed woman makes a good man leave the town,
But a red-head woman makes a boy slap his papa down.

O ashes to ashes and dust to dust,
I said ashes to ashes and dust to dust,
If my blues don't get you my jazzing must.

SECOND HAND ROSE

Words by GRANT CLARKE
Music by JAMES F. HANLEY

283

SAY IT WITH MUSIC

from the 1921 Stage Production MUSIC BOX REVUE
from the 20th Century Fox Motion Picture ALEXANDER'S RAGTIME BAND

Words and Music by
IRVING BERLIN

SENTIMENTAL ME

from the Broadway Musical THE GARRICK GAIETIES

Words by LORENZ HART
Music by RICHARD RODGERS

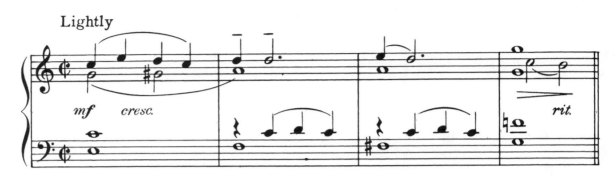

Look at me a - gain, dear; Let's hold hands and then, dear, Sigh in
Dar - ling you're so hand-some, Strong and clev - er and some-times you

cho - rus; It won't bore us, to be sure; ____
seem, dear, Like a dream, dear, that came true. ____

There's no mean-ing to it, Yet we o-ver-do it, With a
That's why I picked you out; Bet-ter men I threw out Of my

rel-ish that is hell-ish to en-dure;
liv-ing room while giv-ing room to you;

I am not the kind that mere-ly flirts;
I would rath-er read of love in books;

I just love and love un-til it hurts.
Love is much more pain-ful than it looks.

291

THE SHEIK OF ARABY

Words by Harry B. SMITH and FRANCIS WHEELER
Music by TED SNYDER

SIDE BY SIDE

Words and Music by
HARRY WOODS

SOMEBODY LOVES ME
from GEORGE WHITE'S SCANDALS OF 1924

Words by B.G. DeSYLVA and BALLARD MacDONALD
Music by GEORGE GERSHWIN
French Version by EMELIA RENAUD

When this world be - gan it was Heav - en's plan.

There should be a girl for ev - 'ry sin - gle man.

To my great re - gret

SOMETIMES I'M HAPPY

Words by CLIFFORD GREY and IRVING CAESAR
Music by VINCENT YOUMANS

307

STARDUST

Words by MITCHELL PARISH
Music by HOAGY CARMICHAEL

Em
E♭dim7
Dm7
G7
C
we're a - part.
You wan - dered down the lane and
F9
E7
far a - way,
leav - ing me a song that will not
A7
Dm
C
Cdim7
3
die.
Love is now the star - dust of yes - ter - day,
3
G7
C
C7♯5
the mu - sic of the years gone by.
Some - times I

THE SONG IS ENDED
(But the Melody Lingers On)

Words and Music by
IRVING BERLIN

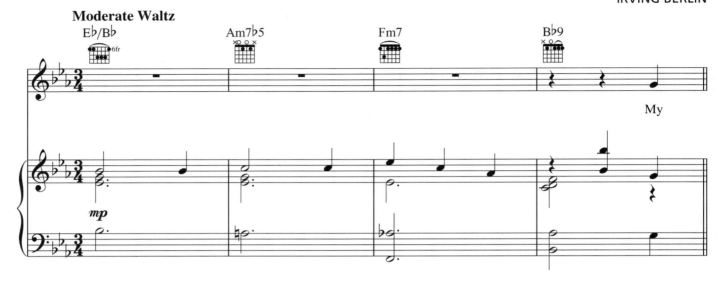

Moderate Waltz

My

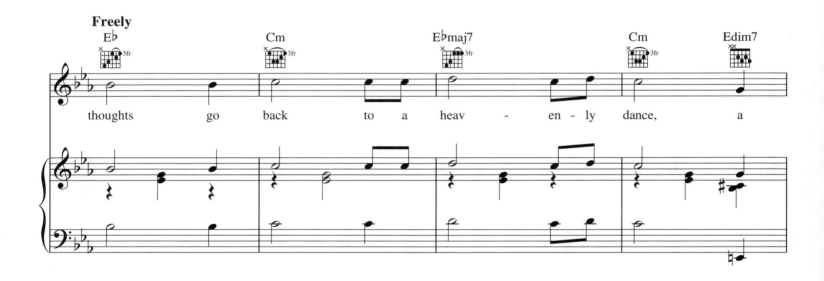

Freely

thoughts go back to a heav - en - ly dance, a

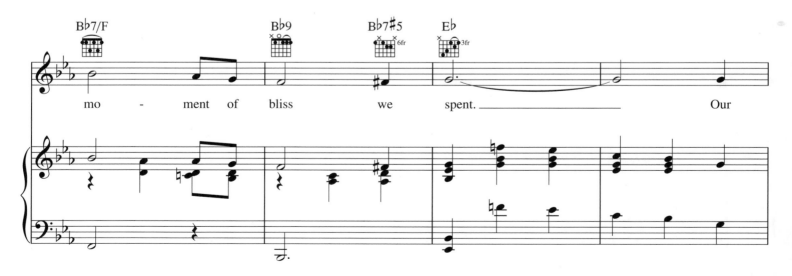

mo - ment of bliss we spent. _____ Our

STOUTHEARTED MEN

from THE NEW MOON

Lyrics by OSCAR HAMMERSTEIN II
Music by SIGMUND ROMBERG

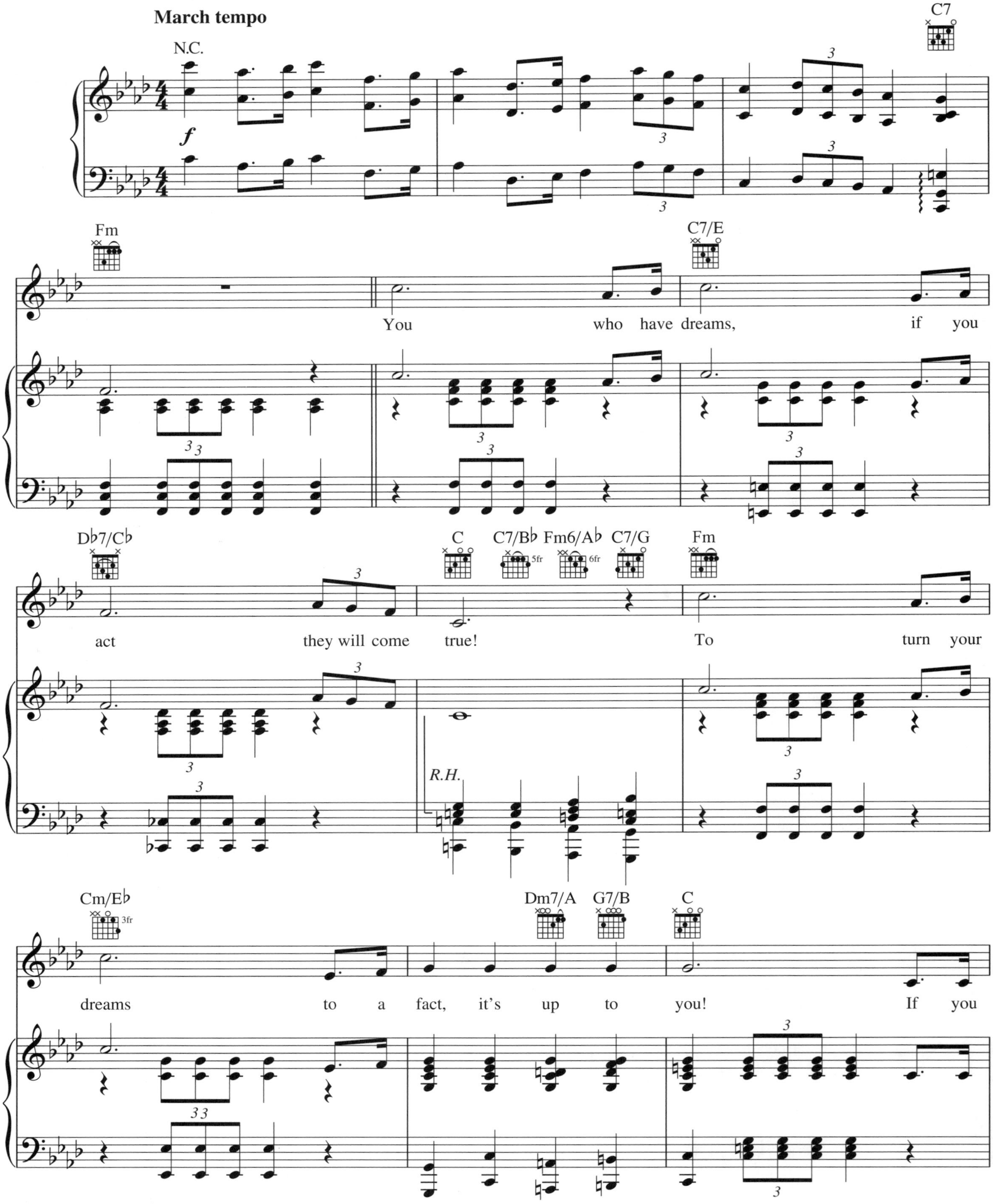

March tempo
N.C.
C7
f
Fm
C7/E
You who have dreams, if you
D♭7/C♭
C
C7/B♭
Fm6/A♭
C7/G
Fm
act they will come true! To turn your
R.H.
Cm/E♭
Dm7/A
G7/B
C
dreams to a fact, it's up to you! If you

SWEET SUE-JUST YOU

from RHYTHM PARADE

Words by WILL J. HARRIS
Music by VICTOR YOUNG

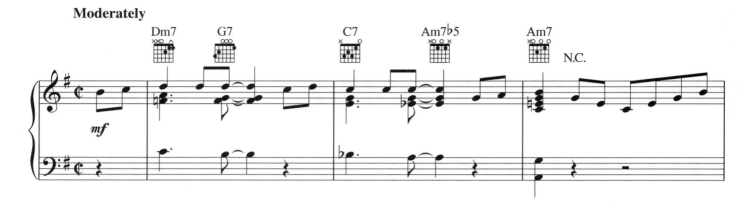

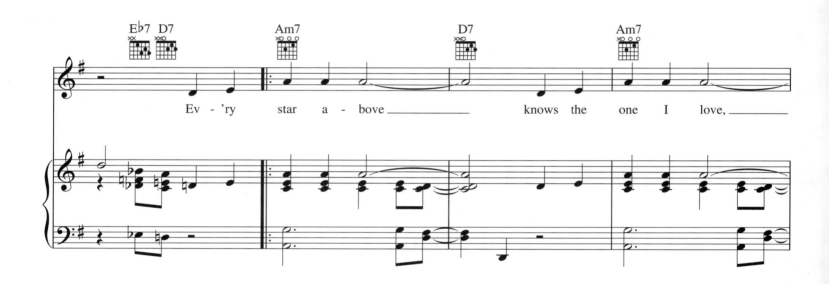

Ev - 'ry star a - bove _____ knows the one I love, _____

_____ sweet Sue, _____ just you. _____

WHEN MY BABY SMILES AT ME

Words and Music by HARRY VON TILZER, ANDREW B. STERLING,
BILL MUNRO and TED LEWIS

THAT'S MY WEAKNESS NOW

Words and Music by
BUD GREEN and SAM STEPT

THOU SWELL

from A CONNECTICUT YANKEE
from WORDS AND MUSIC

Words by LORENZ HART
Music by RICHARD RODGERS

TOOT, TOOT, TOOTSIE!
(Good-Bye!)
from THE JAZZ SINGER

Words and Music by GUS KAHN,
ERNIE ERDMAN, DAN RUSSO and TED FIORITO

'WAY DOWN YONDER
IN NEW ORLEANS

Words and Music by HENRY CREAMER
and J. TURNER LAYTON

WHAT'LL I DO?

from MUSIC BOX REVUE OF 1924

Words and Music by
IRVING BERLIN

Moderate Waltz

Gone is the ro - mance that was so di - vine.
Do you re - mem - ber a night filled with bliss?

'Tis bro - ken and can - not be mend - ed.
The moon - light was soft - ly de - scend - ing.

You must go
Your lips and

WHEN MY SUGAR WALKS DOWN THE STREET

Words and Music by JIMMY MCHUGH,
GENE AUSTIN and IRVING MILLS

347

348

WHEN THE RED, RED ROBIN COMES BOB, BOB BOBBIN' ALONG

from I'LL CRY TOMORROW

Words and Music by
HARRY WOODS

351

WHEN YOU'RE SMILING
(The Whole World Smiles With You)

Words and Music by
MARK FISHER, JOE GOODWIN
and LARRY SHAY

WHO?
from SUNNY

Lyrics by OTTO HARBACH and OSCAR HAMMERSTEIN II
Music by JEROME KERN

WHO'S SORRY NOW

from THREE LITTLE WORDS

Words by BERT KALMAR and HARRY RUBY
Music by TED SNYDER

WHY DO I LOVE YOU?

from SHOW BOAT

Lyrics by OSCAR HAMMERSTEIN II
Music by JEROME KERN

8vb

WITH A SONG IN MY HEART

from SPRING IS HERE

Words by LORENZ HART
Music by RICHARD RODGERS

WITHOUT A SONG

Words by WILLIAM ROSE
and EDWARD ELISCU
Music by VINCENT YOUMANS

YES SIR, THAT'S MY BABY

Lyrics by GUS KAHN
Music by WALTER DONALDSON

374

YES! WE HAVE NO BANANAS

By FRANK SILVER
and IRVING CONN

Moderately

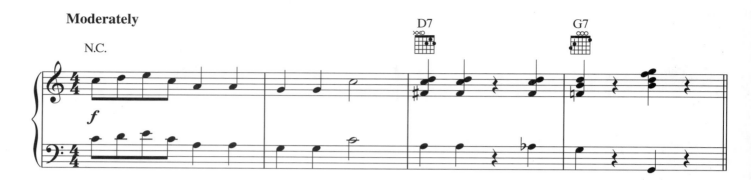

Yes! We have no ba-na-nas. ___ We have no ba-

na-nas to-day. ___ We've string beans and hon-ions, cab-